The Ultimate Christmas

ISBN-13: 978-1494253974

ISBN-10: 1494253976

Introduction

Over the years I have gathered an amazing collection of Christmas cookie recipes - great homemade cookies, full of flavors and memories, loved by family and friends, also easy to prepare with my grandchildren. To keep with tradition, once they are baked and cooled completely, they can be wrapped in colorful paper or air tight containers to make truly festive homemade gifts! A must have for the cookie baker! Book features lots of old favorites as well as new recipes.

These cookies went so fast, the kids got into my cookies I had set aside to photograph.

ANISE COOKIES

¾ cup butter, softened

1 cup sugar

1 egg

½ teaspoon Pure Vanilla Extract

2 teaspoons baking powder

½ teaspoon salt

2 cups sifted flour

1½ teaspoons Anise Seed

½ cup finely chopped pecans, optional

1½ cups confectioners' sugar

1½ to 2 Tablespoons milk or water

¼ teaspoon anise oil or extract for flavor

Directions

1. In a large bowl beat butter and sugar in large bowl with electric mixer on medium speed until light and fluffy. Add egg and vanilla; mix well. Add baking powder and salt to sifted flour; stir with wire whisk. Gradually add dry ingredients and anise seed to butter mixture, beating well after each addition.

2. Shape dough into log, about 1½ inches in diameter and 12 inches long. Wrap in wax paper or plastic wrap. Refrigerate at least 2 hours.

3. Preheat oven to 400 degrees F. Cut log into thin slices and place 1 inch apart on greased baking sheets.

4. Bake 8 minutes or until golden brown. Cool on baking sheets 1 minute. Remove to wire racks; cool completely.

5. Blend together powdered sugar, milk and anise extract for extra flavor.

Makes 28 to 30 Cookies

SUGAR COOKIE LOG

This recipe makes a beautiful pinwheel cookie. Try different flavors instead of vanilla; such as anise or lemon with yellow instead of green coloring. They work out better when cut thin, before baking, but they are worth the effort.

3 cups (375g) all-purpose flour

1/2 teaspoon baking powder

1/2 teaspoon salt

1 cup (226g) (2 sticks) unsalted butter

1 1/3 (267g) cups sugar

2 large eggs

2 teaspoons vanilla extract

Green food coloring

Sprinkles

Directions:

1. In a medium bowl, sift together the flour, baking powder and salt.

2. In the bowl of a stand mixer fitted with the paddle attachment, or a hand mixer works too; beat the butter until smooth, about 2 minutes. Add the sugar and continue beating until the mixture is light and fluffy, about 3 minutes. Add the eggs one at a time, beating between each addition, then add the vanilla.

3. Turn the mixer off; if using. Add the flour and then beat just until combined. Remove the dough and separate it into two equal pieces. Shape one piece of the dough into an 8-inch square, wrap it securely in plastic wrap and place it in the fridge. (This will be the white portion of the cookies.)

4. Return the remaining piece of dough to the stand mixer bowl, and with the mixer on "low," add in the green food coloring, drop by drop, until it reaches your desired pink color. Remove the pink dough, shape it into an 8-inch square, wrap it securely in plastic wrap and place it in the fridge. Refrigerate the dough for 30 minutes.

5. Remove the dough from the fridge and cut each square in half to form two rectangles. Wrap half of each color of dough in plastic wrap and return it to the fridge. Place the white dough in between two pieces of wax paper and roll it into a rectangle about 1/8-inch thick. Roll out the green dough between two separate pieces of wax paper until it is a rectangle about 1/8-inch thick.

6. Peel the top layer of wax paper off of the white dough and then peel the wax paper off one side of the green dough and use the other side to transfer the green dough on top of the white dough. Very lightly roll the two layers together. If the dough cracks; gently Pinch it together again.

7. Starting at the shorter end of the rectangle, roll the dough as tightly as possible into a log. Repeat the rolling and stacking process with the remaining dough in the fridge. Wrap the logs in wax paper and then plastic wrap and refrigerate them for 1 hour.

8. Remove the dough logs and roll them on the counter several times so they don't develop a flat side. Unwrap the dough logs and place the sprinkles in a large, shallow dish. Roll the dough logs in the sprinkles until they are completely coated. Re-wrap the dough logs in wax paper and plastic and refrigerate them for 4 more hours.

9. When ready to bake, preheat the oven to 350ºF and line two baking sheets with parchment paper. Remove the dough from the fridge and slice each log into 1/4-inch rounds. Place the rounds about 2 inches apart on the baking sheets, as the cookies will expand when baked.

10. Bake the cookies for 10 to 12 minutes until pale golden, and then transfer them to a rack to cool completely.

Makes about 30 cookies

JAM FILLED COOKIES

Filled with jam and rolled in chopped nuts, these thumbprints are easy, delicious and very pretty.

2/3 cup (168g) unsalted butter, at room temperature

1/3 cup (67g) granulated sugar

2 large egg yolks

1 teaspoon vanilla extract

1/2 teaspoon salt

1 ½ (185g) cups all-purpose flour

2 large egg whites

3/4 cup (96g) finely chopped nuts of choice

1/3 cup (30g) jam (any flavor)

1. Preheat oven to 350 F. Line baking sheets with parchment paper or a non-stick baking mat.

2. In a large bowl, beat together butter and sugar until light and fluffy. Beat in egg yolks, vanilla extract and salt. Gradually stir in flour. Form dough into 1-inch diameter balls. Dip in lightly beaten egg whites, then roll in nuts. Place 1 inch apart on prepared cookie sheets. Press down center of each with thumb.

3. Bake for 16 to 18 minutes, or until golden brown. Cool on baking sheet for 5 minutes, then transfer to a wire rack to cool completely. Just before serving, fill centers of cookies with jam. Or, fill centers with 1/2 teaspoon of jam before baking.

Makes about 24 cookies

SHORTCAKE BITES

1 ¼ cups (155g) all-purpose flour

3 Tablespoons sugar

½ cup (1 stick) (113g) butter, cold, cut into pieces

1 Tablespoon red and green nonpareils or sprinkles or ½ cup mini baking bits

Directions

1. In food processor with knife blade attached, pulse flour and sugar until combined. Add butter and pulse until dough begins to come together. Place dough in medium bowl. With hand, gently knead in nonpareils or baking bits until evenly blended and dough forms a ball.

2. On lightly floured waxed paper, pat dough into 8" by 5" rectangle; freeze 15 minutes. Cut dough into 1/2-inch squares. Place squares, ½-inch apart, on ungreased large cookie sheet.

3. Preheat oven to 325 degrees F.

4. Bake cookies 18 to 20 minutes or until lightly browned on bottom. Transfer cookies to wire rack to cool. Store cookies in tightly covered container at room temperature up to 1 week, or in freezer up to 3 months.

CHRISTMAS ORNAMENT COOKIES

2 ¼ cups (280g) all-purpose flour

¼ teaspoon salt

1 cup (200g) sugar

¾ cup (170g) butter, softened

1 large egg

1 teaspoon vanilla extract

1 teaspoon almond extract

Icing: 2 cups (250g) powdered sugar

2 Tablespoons milk or lemon juice

Food coloring, optional

Directions

1. In a medium bowl, combine flour and salt; stir to blend. In a large bowl, beat sugar and butter with an electric mixer at medium speed until light and fluffy. Beat in egg, vanilla and almond extract. Gradually add the flour mixture. Beat at low speed until well blended. Divide dough in half; cover and refrigerate 30 minutes or until firm.

2. Preheat oven to 350 degrees F. Working with 1 half at a time, roll out dough on lightly floured surface to ¼-inch thick.

3. Cut dough into desired shapes with assorted floured cookie cutters. Reroll trimmings and cut out more cookies. Place cut-out cookies on

ungreased baking sheets. Using drinking straw or tip of a Sharpe knife, cut hole near top of each cookie to allow for piece of ribbon or string to be inserted for hanger, if desired. Bake 10 to 12 minutes or until edges are golden brown. Let cookies stand on baking sheet 1 minutes. Transfer to wire racks, cook completely.

4. Prepare Icing: Place powdered sugar and milk in a small bowl; stir with a spoon until smooth. (Icing will be very thick)If it is too thick; stir in 1 teaspoon additional milk. Divide into small bowls and tint with food coloring, if desired.

5. Spoon icing into a small resealable plastic storage bag; cutoff very tiny corner of bag; pipe icing decoratively over cookies as desired. Decorate with candies as desired. Let stand at room temperature 40 minutes or until set. Thread ribbon through each cookie hole to hang as a Christmas tree ornament.

Makes about 24 cookies

CHOCOLATE PRETZELS

1 package square pretzels

1 package milk chocolate kisses

Candy coated plain chocolate candy or Red Hot's

Directions

Preheat oven to 200 degrees F. Place pretzels on cookie sheet. Place 1 milk chocolate kiss in center of each pretzel. Warm in 200 degrees F oven for 3-5 minutes or until soft enough to press candies into kiss and flatten into pretzel.

MARASCHINO CHERRY COOKIES

2 jars (10-oz each) maraschino cherries

½ cup (120g) butter or margarine, softened

1 cup (200g) granulated sugar

1 egg

1 ½ teaspoon vanilla extract

1 ½ cups (180g) all-purpose flour

½ cup (59g) unsweetened cocoa powder

¼ teaspoon salt

½ teaspoon baking powder

½ cup (85g) semisweet chocolate chips

2 Tablespoons milk

Directions

1. Preheat oven to 350 degrees F.

2. Drain maraschino cherries, reserving 1 teaspoon juice. In a medium bowl, place butter and sugar. Beat with an electric mixer on medium speed 3 to 4 minutes, or until well blended. Add egg and vanilla; mix well.

3. Combine flour, cocoa, salt and baking powder; add flour mixture to butter mixture. Beat until well mixed.

4. In a small saucepan place the chocolate chips and milk. Heat, stirring constantly, over low heat until chocolate melts. Stir in reserved maraschino cherry juice. Let cool slightly.

5. Shape dough into 1-inch balls. Place on an ungreased baking sheet. Push in center with your thumb; spoon 1 teaspoon chocolate mixture into each thumbprint and top with a cherry.

6. Bake in preheated oven 10 to 12 minutes, or until cookies are firm. Transfer to wire racks. Let cool completely. Store in an airtight container

PUMPKIN OATMEAL COOKIES

1 ½ (185g) cup flour

1 cup (200g) sugar

½ teaspoon baking soda

¼ teaspoon nutmeg

¾ teaspoon cinnamon

1 teaspoon salt

¾ cup shortening

1 egg, beaten

1 cup canned pumpkin

1 ¾ cup rolled oats

1 cup (180g) Raisins or Chopped Nuts

Directions

1. Preheat oven to 400 degrees.

2. In a mixing bowl, stir together flour, sugar, baking soda, cinnamon, nutmeg and salt. Add and mix shortening. Stir until mixture is crumbly.
3. Stir in egg, pumpkin, oats and raisins (or nuts). Drop teaspoonful of dough onto an ungreased cookie sheet. 4. Bake 15 minutes or until done.

PUMPKIN CRÈME PIES

2 1/3 (270g) cups all-purpose flour

2 teaspoons baking soda

½ teaspoon salt

1 Tablespoon pumpkin pie spice

8 Tablespoons unsalted butter, room temperature

1 cup light brown sugar, packed

¼ cup molasses

2/3 cup pure pumpkin puree

1 large egg

½ cup (100g) granulated sugar, for rolling

Filling

1 (8-oz) package cream cheese, softened

3 ½ cups powdered sugar, sifted

1 teaspoon vanilla extract

Directions:

1. Whisk together the flour, baking soda, salt, and pumpkin pie spice.

2. Working with a stand mixer, preferably fitted with a paddle attachment, or a hand mixer in a large bowl, beat the butter on medium speed until smooth and creamy. Add the brown sugar, molasses, and pumpkin puree and beat for 2 minutes, scraping down the sides of the bowl as needed. Add the egg and beat for 1 minute more.

3. Reduce the mixer speed to low and add the dry ingredients, mixing until the flour and spices disappear. If flour remains in the bottom of the bowl, mix the last of the dry ingredients by hand to avoid over beating. The dough will be very soft.

4. Divide the dough in half and wrap each piece in plastic wrap. Freeze for at least 30 minutes, or refrigerate for at least 1 hour. If the dough is still sticky, freeze a little longer.

5. Preheat oven to 350°F. Line 2 baking sheets with parchment paper.

6. Put the sugar in a small bowl. Working with one half of dough at a time, divide it into 24 pieces (or use a small cookie scoop), and roll each piece into a ball. Roll the balls in the sugar, then place dough balls on prepared cookie sheets and use the bottom of a glass to ever-so-gently press down on the cookies. Do not over crowd.

7. Bake the cookies one sheet at a time for 7-9 minutes, or until the top feels set to the touch. Let cookies cool 5 minutes on the sheets before transferring them to a wire rack. Repeat with second batch of dough.

Filling

1. In a medium bowl with an electric mixer, combine cream cheese and powdered sugar. Mix on low speed until the sugar is blended, increase speed to medium-high and mix for about one minute. Add in vanilla and continue mixing on low speed until vanilla in fully blended.

2. To assemble the cookies, pipe or spread the filling on the bottom of one cookie. Top with another cookie and press together gently to create a sandwich cookie. Repeat with remaining cookies.

HOLLY COOKIES

6 Tablespoons (84g) margarine

32 regular sized marshmallows

1 teaspoon green food coloring

1 teaspoon vanilla

3 cups (75g) corn flakes

90 red cinnamon candies

Directions:

1. Melt margarine and the 32 marshmallows together in a pan over low heat. Stir as needed.

2. Once the marshmallows have all melted, remove pot from heat and stir in the green food coloring and the vanilla. Stir until the marshmallow mixture is a uniform green color (no streaks).

3. Fold the cornflakes into the marshmallow mixture and stir until all are coated.

4. Drop by teaspoon full onto aluminum foil or parchment paper and place 3 red cinnamon candies in the center of each cookie. Let dry.

CHOCOLATE-PEANUT FILLED COOKIES

1 ½ cups (180g) flour

½ cup (60g) unsweetened cocoa

½ teaspoon baking soda

½ cup sugar

½ cup (90g) brown sugar, packed

½ cup (113g) butter or coconut oil

¼ cup (60g) peanut butter

1 teaspoon vanilla

1egg

Filling

¾ cup peanut butter

¾ cup powdered sugar

½ teaspoon vanilla extract

Directions:

1. Preheat oven to 375 degrees F.

2. In a small bowl, combine flour, cocoa, and baking soda. In a large bowl, beat sugar, brown sugar, and butter until well blended. Blend in ¼ cup peanut butter to mixture. Add vanilla and egg, beat well. Add flour mixture until blended. Set aside.

3. In a small bowl, combine filling ingredients, blending well. Roll filling into 30 ½-inch balls. For each cookie, with floured hands shape 1 Tablespoon dough around 1 peanut butter ball, covering completely.

4. Place cookies 2 inches apart on an ungreased cookie sheet. Flatten with the bottom of a glass dipped in sugar.

Bake in preheated oven for 7 to 9 minutes or until set and slightly cracked. Cool on wire racks. Makes 30 cookies

CHEWY MOLASSES COOKIES

½ cup (120g) unsalted butter, softened

¼ cup olive oil or coconut oil

¼ cup dark molasses

1 cup (180g) brown sugar, packed

1 egg

2-inch piece of fresh ginger, finely grated

2 ¼ (270g) cup flour

½ teaspoon salt

2 teaspoons baking soda

1 teaspoon cinnamon

1 teaspoon ground ginger

1/8 teaspoon black pepper

Granulated sugar, for rolling

Directions

1. Preheat the oven to 350 degrees F. Line two large, heavy baking sheets with parchment paper.

3. In a mixer bowl, at medium speed cream the butter with the olive oil, molasses, and brown sugar. When it is fluffy and lightened, add the egg and whip until smooth. Blend in the grated ginger and its juice.

4. Add the flour, salt, baking soda, cinnamon, ground ginger, and black pepper to the butter mixture. Blend at low speed until thoroughly

combined. The dough will be quite soft. Put the dough in the fridge for at least 30 minutes, or up to 3 days. (This dough can also be wrapped and frozen. Thaw completely in the refrigerator before proceeding with the recipe.)

5. Pour about ½ cup of granulated sugar into a shallow dish. When the dough is stiff enough to handle, separate it roughly into four parts. Divide the first part into 12 walnut-sized chunks of dough, and roll each into a ball. Roll the ball lightly in the sugar, then place on the baking sheet. Repeat for the others, and the second quarter of the dough.

6. Bake the first two sheets of cookies for 12 minutes, swapping each baking sheet from the upper to lower rack (and vice versa) at the 6-minute mark. Remove and let cool for 5 minutes, transfer the cookies with a spatula to wire racks.

7. Repeat with remaining dough. While the remainder of the cookies cool, make the glaze. Dribble the glaze over the cookies in a thin swirl, using a fork, or paint it on with a pastry brush. Let the glaze dry and cool on the cookies until hard. Store the cookies in an airtight container for up to a week.

Lemon glaze:

1/4 cup (60ml) fresh lemon juice

1/3 cup (70g) granulated sugar

1 cup (120g) powdered sugar

Whisk the lemon juice together with the granulated and powdered sugars. Frost immediately.

Makes 48 cookies

ALMOND SPRITZ COOKIES

2 cups (480g) unsalted butter, softened

1 1/3 (270) cups sugar

1 teaspoon pure vanilla extract

½ teaspoons almond extract

3 2/3 (440g) cups all-purpose flour

½ teaspoon salt

1 cup almond flour (almond meal)

9oz (250g) semisweet or milk chocolate, coarsely chopped

Directions:

1. Preheat the oven to 350°F (180°C). Line 3 large baking sheets with parchment paper.

2. Beat the butter in a large bowl with an electric mixer set on high speed until smooth. Gradually beat in the sugar, and beat 2 minutes, until light and fluffy. Beat in the vanilla and almond extracts. On low speed, beat in about two-thirds of the flour and the salt. Stir in the almond flour and the remaining flour. Knead in the bowl until smooth.

3. Fit a pastry bag with a ¾-inch (2cm) wide star tip. In batches, transfer the dough to the bag. Pipe out 3-inch (7.5cm) lengths of the dough; twist them to make a horseshoe shape, bringing the ends close together; spacing them 1-inch (2.5cm) apart onto the baking sheets.

Bake 12-15 minutes until golden. Transfer to a wire rack to cool, but reserve the parchment-lined baking sheets.

4. Melt the chocolate in a small bowl placed in a pan of barely simmering water, taking care not to splash any water into the chocolate. Dip the ends of the cookies into the melted chocolate, and return to the baking sheets to cool and set the chocolate; decorate with sprinkles if desired.

Store in an airtight container for 2-3 days.

GINGERBREAD MEN

1/2 (120g) cup butter, softened

3/4 cup (135g) packed dark brown sugar

1/3 cup molasses

1 large Egg

2 tablespoons water

2 2/3 cups (320g) all-purpose flour

2 teaspoons ground ginger

1 teaspoon baking soda

1/2 teaspoon salt

 1/2 teaspoon each ground cinnamon, nutmeg and allspice

Directions

1. In a large bowl, cream butter and brown sugar until light and fluffy. Beat in the molasses, egg and water. Combine the flour, ginger, baking soda, salt, cinnamon, nutmeg and allspice; add to creamed mixture and mix well. Divide dough in half. Refrigerate for 30 minutes or until easy to handle.

2. On a lightly floured surface, roll out each portion of dough to 1/8-in. thickness. Cut with a floured 4-in. cookie cutter. Place 2-inches apart on greased baking sheets. Reroll scraps.

3. Bake at 350° for 8-10 minutes or until edges are firm. Remove to wire racks to cool completely. Decorate as desired. Makes about 24 gingerbread men depending on size

FRUITCAKE COOKIES

¾ cup (170g) sugar

½ cup (120g) butter, softened

1 egg

½ (120ml) cup milk

2 Tablespoons orange juice

1 Tablespoon vinegar

2 cups all-purpose flour

1 teaspoon baking powder

½ teaspoon baking soda

¼ teaspoon salt

½ (75g) cup chopped walnuts

½ cup (75g) candied mixed fruit

½ cup raisins

¼ cup chopped dried pineapple

Powdered sugar

1. Preheat oven to 350 degrees F. Grease cookie sheets. In a large bowl beat sugar and butter. Beat in egg, milk, orange juice and vinegar until blended. Mix in flour, baking powder, baking soda and salt. Stir in walnuts, mixed fruit, raisins and pineapple. Drop by rounded Tablespoons of dough 2-inches apart onto prepared cookie sheets.

2. Bake 12 to 14 minutes until lightly browned around edges. Cool 2 minutes on cookie sheets. Transfer to wire racks; cool completely. Dust with powdered sugar. Store in air tight container.

 Makes about 30 cookies

STRAWBERRY SHORTCAKE COOKIES

2 cups diced fresh strawberries

1 teaspoon fresh lemon juice

½ cup (100g) plus 1 Tablespoon granulated sugar

2 cups (240g) all-purpose flour

2 teaspoons baking powder

½ teaspoon coarse salt

6 Tablespoons cold unsalted butter, cut into small pieces

2/3 cup (160ml) heavy cream

Turbinado sugar, for sprinkling

Directions:

1. Preheat oven to 375 degrees. Line a baking sheet with parchment paper and set aside.

2. Combine strawberries, lemon juice, and 2 tablespoons granulated sugar. Whisk together flour, baking powder, salt, and remaining 7 Tablespoons granulated sugar in a large bowl. Cut in the butter with a pastry cutter, or rub in with your fingers, until mixture resembles coarse crumbs. Stir in cream until dough starts to come together, then stir in strawberry mixture.

3. Using a 1½-inch ice cream scoop or a Tablespoon, drop cookie dough onto prepared baking sheet, spacing evenly apart. Sprinkle cookies with turbinado sugar, and bake until golden brown, about 22 to 25 minutes. Transfer to a wire rack, and let cool.

Note-Cookies are best served immediately, but can be stored in an airtight container at room temperature for up to 1 day.

CHOCOLATE PEPPERMINT COOKIES

A glass of cold milk and freshly baked chocolate peppermint cookies makes an unbeatable afternoon snack.

½ cup (113g) margarine, or butter, softened

½ cup (100g) sugar

½ cup (90g) firmly packed brown sugar

½ cup frozen egg substitute, thawed

1 teaspoon vanilla extract

2 ¼ cups all-purpose flour

1 teaspoon baking powder

¼ teaspoon baking soda

¼ teaspoon salt

¼ cup (30g) plus 1 Tablespoon unsweetened cocoa

2/3 cup finely crushed peppermint candies (about 30 candies)

Vegetable cooking spray

Directions

1. Beat margarine with an electric mixer at medium speed until creamy; gradually add white and brown sugars, beating well. Add egg substitute and vanilla; beat well.

2. Combine flour, baking powder, baking soda, salt and cocoa. Add to margarine mixture, stirring until just blended. Stir in crushed candy. Drop dough by level Tablespoonful's, 2-inches apart, on cookie sheets sprayed with vegetable spray.

3. Bake at 350 degrees F for 10 to 12 minutes. Remove from cookie sheets, let cool on wire racks

Makes 44 cookies

THIN MINT COOKIES

Chocolate Cookie Wafers

1 (18¼ oz.) package fudge cake mix

3 Tablespoons shortening, melted

½ cup cake flour, measured then sifted

1 egg

3 Tablespoons water

Nonstick cooking spray

Coating

3 (12-oz.) bags semi-sweet chocolate chips

¾ teaspoon peppermint extract

6 Tablespoons shortening (Coconut oil also works well)

Directions

1. Combine chocolate wafer ingredients in a bowl until well blended.

2. On a surface lightly dusted with flour, shape dough into two logs, about 1½ inches (or about 4 cm) in diameter.

3. Wrap in plastic wrap, waxed paper or parchment and freeze for at least 1to 2 hours, until dough is very firm and can be sliced into wafers.

4. Preheat oven to 375 degrees F.

5. Slice dough into rounds not more than ¼-inch thick - if they are too thick, they will not be as crisp - and place on a parchment lined baking sheet.

6. These cookies are firm and will not spread very much, so you can put them quite close together.

7. Bake for 13-15 minutes, until cookies are firm at the edges. Cool cookies completely on a wire rack before dipping in chocolate

8. Chocolate Coating: Combine chocolate chips with peppermint extract and shortening in a large microwave-safe glass or ceramic bowl.

9. Heat on 50 percent power for 2 minutes, stir gently, and then heat for an addition minute. Stir once again, and if chocolate is not a smooth consistency, continue to zap in microwave in 30-second intervals until smooth.

10. Use a fork to dip each wafer in the chocolate, tap the fork on the edge of the bowl so that the excess chocolate runs off, and then place the cookies side-by-side on a wax paper-lined baking sheet. Refrigerate until firm.

Makes about 100 cookies

LEMON SUGAR COOKIES

2 ¾ cups (340g) all-purpose flour

½ teaspoon baking soda

1 teaspoon baking powder

½ teaspoon salt

1 cup (240g) butter, softened

1 ½ (300g) cups white sugar

1 egg

½ teaspoon vanilla extract

Zest of one large lemon, finely minced

4 Tablespoons fresh lemon juice

½ cup (100g) sugar for rolling cookies

Directions:

1. Preheat oven to 350 degrees F. Line cookie sheets with parchment paper.

2. In a small bowl, whisk together flour, baking soda, baking powder and salt. Set aside. Using a mixer, beat together the butter and sugar until smooth and very fluffy.

3. Beat in egg, vanilla extract, lemon juice and lemon zest. Gradually blend in the dry ingredients. Roll rounded teaspoonful of dough into balls, and roll in sugar. Place on lined cookie sheets about 1½ inches apart.

4. Bake 8 to 10 minutes in the preheated oven, or until lightly browned. Let stand on cookie sheet two minutes before removing to cool on wire racks.

SNOWMEN COOKIES

1 (8-oz-226g) pkg. Cream Cheese, softened

1 cup (125g) powdered sugar

¾ cup (1 ½ sticks) Butter or margarine

1 teaspoon vanilla

2 ½ (310g) cups flour

½ teaspoon baking soda

Sifted powdered sugar

Miniature peanut butter cups (optional)

Directions

1. Mix cream cheese, 1 cup powdered sugar, butter and vanilla with an electric mixer on medium speed until well blended. Add flour and baking soda; mix well.

2. Shape dough into equal number of ½ -inch and 1-inch diameter balls. Using 1 small and 1 large ball for each snowman, place balls, slightly overlapping, on ungreased cookie sheets. Flatten to ¼ -inch thickness with bottom of glass dipped in additional flour. Repeat with remaining balls.

3. Bake at 325 degrees F. for 19 to 21 minutes or until light golden brown. Cool on wire racks. Sprinkle each snowman with sifted powdered sugar. Decorate with icing as desired. Cut peanut butter cups in half for hats. Makes about 3 dozen

GRANOLA MERINGUE COOKIES

Store these sweet treats in an air tight container to keep then crisp.

3 egg whites

½ teaspoon cream of tartar

¼ cup (50g) plus 2 Tablespoons sugar

¾ cup (68g) granola cereal without raisins

¼ teaspoon vanilla extract

¼ teaspoon almond extract

Directions

1. Line 2 baking sheets with parchment paper; set aside

2. Beat eggs whites and cream of tartar; with an electric mixer on high speed until foamy. Gradually add sugar, 1 Tablespoon at a time, beating until stiff peaks form and sugar dissolves (2 to 4 minutes) Fold in cereal, vanilla and almond extracts.

3. Drop mixture by level Tablespoonful 2 inches apart onto prepared baking sheets. Bake at 225 degrees F. for 1 hour and 10 minutes. Turn oven off. Cool in oven for 2 hours with the oven door closed. Carefully remove cookies from paper; let cool completely on wire racks.

Makes 4 dozen cookies

MARSHMALLOW MUD SQUARES

2 cups sugar

1 cup (120g) shortening

4 eggs

3 teaspoons vanilla

1½ cups (180g) flour

1/3 cup (56g) cocoa powder

1/3 teaspoon salt

1 (6½-oz.) bag mini marshmallows

For the frosting:

2 sticks butter, room temperature

½ cup (60g) cocoa powder

4 cups powdered sugar

1 teaspoon vanilla

½ cup evaporated milk

1. Preheat the oven to 300 degrees F. In the bowl of an electric mixer, add sugar and shortening; beat until creamy. Add eggs and vanilla and beats 30 seconds. In a separate bowl, sift the flour, cocoa and salt together. Add to the mixture and beat until well combined. Pour the mixture into a greased and floured 9 x 13-inch glass baking dish. Bake for 35 minutes, or when toothpick inserted comes out clean.

2. Make the frosting: In the bowl of an electric mixer, beat butter, cocoa, powdered sugar and vanilla. Gradually add the milk; until smooth. Set aside.

3. Remove cake from the oven. Spread the marshmallows on top of the cake and return the pan to the oven for 5 more minutes. Remove the pan from the oven and cool for a few minutes. Evenly apply the frosting. Allow this to stand about 2 hours before cutting into squares.

Note: If the marshmallows are too hot, the frosting will sink right through. The frosting should be the top layer. It will darken once it hits the heat of the cake.

FROSTED PUMPKIN SQUARES
¾ cup (1½ sticks) butter or margarine

2 cups (400g) granulated sugar

1 (16-oz) can pumpkin puree

4 eggs

2 cups (500g) flour

2 teaspoons baking powder

1 teaspoon ground cinnamon

½ teaspoon baking powder

½ teaspoon salt

¼ teaspoon ground nutmeg

1 cup (150g) chopped walnuts

Frosting

1 (8-oz 226g) Cream Cheese, softened

1/3 cup (80g) butter or margarine

1 teaspoon vanilla

3 cups sifted powdered sugar

Directions

1. Mix butter and sugar with electric mixer on medium speed until light and fluffy. Blend in pumpkin and eggs. Mix in combined dry ingredients. Stir in walnuts.

2. Spread into greased 15x10x1-inch baking pan

3. Bake at 350 degrees F. for 30 to 35 minutes or until toothpick inserted in center comes out clean; cool

Frosting

Mix: Cream cheese, butter and vanilla in large bowl with electric mixer until creamy. Gradually add sugar, mixing well after each addition. Spread on cake. Cut into squares.

Makes 24 Bars

APPLE CRUMB SQUARES

2 cups (90g) oats (quick cooking or old fashioned) uncooked

1 ½ (200g) cups all-purpose flour

1 cup (180g) packed brown sugar

¾ cup (170g) butter or margarine, melted

1 teaspoon ground cinnamon

½ teaspoon baking soda

½ teaspoon salt, optional

¼ teaspoon ground nutmeg

1 cup applesauce

½ cup (75g) chopped nuts

Directions

1. Preheat oven to 350 degrees F.

2. In a large bowl, combine all ingredients; except apple sauce and nuts; mix until crumbly. Reserve 1 cup oat mixture. Press remaining mixture on bottom of a greased 13x9-inch baking dish. Bake 13 to 15 minutes; cool. Spread applesauce over partially baked crust; sprinkle with nuts. Sprinkle reserved 1-cup oats mixture over top. Bake 14 to 15 minutes or until golden brown. Cool in pan on wire rack; cut into 2-inch squares

Makes 24 squares

CREAMY LEMON BARS

1 pkg. (2-layer size) Lemon cake mix

3 large eggs, divided

½ cup oil

2 (8-oz) pkg. cream cheese, softened

1 (8-oz) container Sour cream

½ cup sugar

1 teaspoon grated lemon peel

1 Tablespoon Lemon juice

Powdered sugar

Directions

1. Mix cake mix, 1 egg and oil. Press mixture onto bottom and up sides of lightly greased 15x10x1-inch baking pan. Bake at 350 degrees F for 10 minutes.

2. Mix cream cheese with electric mixer on medium speed until smooth. Add remaining 2 eggs, sour cream, sugar, lemon peel and juice; mix until blended. Pour batter over crust.

3. Bake at 350 degrees F. for 30 to 35 minutes or until filling is just set in center and edges are light golden brown. Cool. Sprinkle with powdered sugar. Cut into bars. Store leftover bars in refrigerator

Makes 24 Bar.

PEANUTTY CHOCOLATE CHIP BARS

1 cup chunky or creamy peanut butter

1 cup packed brown sugar

2/3 cup light or dark corn syrup

½ cup butter or margarine (Coconut oil works too)

2 eggs

1 teaspoon vanilla extract

2½ cups flour

1½ teaspoons baking powder

½ teaspoon salt

2 cups (12-oz) semisweet chocolate chips, divided

Directions

1. Preheat oven to 350 degrees F.

In a large bowl with mixer at medium speed, beat peanut butter, brown sugar, corn syrup, butter, eggs and vanilla until smooth. Reduce speed; beat in flour, baking powder and salt until well blended. Stir in 1½ cups chocolate chips.

2. Bake 25 minutes or until lightly browned. Cool completely on wire rack.

3. In a heavy saucepan over low heat, stir remaining ½ cup chocolate chips until melted and smooth. Drizzle over surface; cool before cutting. Makes 48 bars

CHIPPY CHEWY BARS

½ cup (1stick) Butter or margarine

1½ cups graham cracker crumbs

1 (10-oz) pkg. Peanut butter chips, divided

1½ cups sweetened coconut flakes

1 (14-oz) can sweetened condensed milk

1 cup (160g) semisweet chocolate chips

1½ teaspoons shortening

Directions

1. Heat oven to 350 degrees F.

2. Place butter in 13x9x2-inch baking pan. Heat in oven until melted; remove pan from oven. Sprinkle graham cracker crumbs evenly over butter; press down with fork. Sprinkle 1 cup peanut butter chips over crumbs; sprinkle coconut over chips. Layer remaining 2/3 cup peanut butter chips over coconut; drizzle sweetened condensed milk evenly over top. Press down firmly.

3. Bake 20 minutes or until lightly browned. Combine chocolate chips and shortening in small microwave-safe bowl. Microwave at medium for 1 minute; stir. If necessary, microwave at high an additional 15 seconds at a time, stirring after each heating, just until chips are melted and mixture is smooth. Drizzle evenly over top of baked mixture. Cool completely. Cut into 48 bars.

Makes 48 bars

EASY LINZER BARS

2 cups (500g) flour

½ cup sugar

¾ teaspoon baking soda

½ teaspoon cinnamon

½ teaspoon grated lemon peel

½ cup (1 stick) margarine or butter

¼ cup light corn syrup

½ cup seedless raspberry preserves

1/3 cup (50g) finely chopped walnuts

2/3 cup (90g) powdered sugar

1 Tablespoon milk

Directions

1. Preheat oven to 350 degrees F.

2. In a large bowl combine flour, sugar, baking soda, cinnamon and lemon peel. In a small saucepan heat margarine and corn syrup over low heat until margarine melts. Stir into flour mixture until blended, Divide dough into 5 equal pieces.

3. On a large ungreased cookie sheet, pat each piece of dough into 14 x 1-inch rope

4. Combine raspberry preserves and walnuts. Make an indentation down the center of each rope; fill with preserve mixture, mounding slightly.

5. Bake 12 to 14 minutes or until lightly browned. Remove from oven; immediately cut diagonally into 1-inch-wide slices.

In a small bowl combine powdered sugar and milk; stir until smooth. Drizzle over warm cookies. Cool on wire racks. Store in airtight container.

Makes about 5 dozen cookies

COOKIE BAR CRUST

This recipe is the basic cookie bar crust in the following recipes

Cooking Spray

2 cups (250g) flour

½ cup (1stick) cold butter cut into pieces

1/3 (67g) cup sugar

¼ teaspoon salt

Directions

1. Preheat oven to 350 degrees F. Spray 13 x 9-inch baking pan with cooking spray.

2. In a large bowl with mixer at medium speed, beat flour, butter, sugar and salt until mixture resembles coarse crumbs. Press firmly into bottom and ¼-inch up sides of prepared pan.

3. Bake 15 minutes or until golden brown. Top with desired filling. Complete as recipe directs.

PECAN PIE BARS

Bar cookie Crust (Recipe page 39)

2 eggs

¾ cup (225g) light or dark corn syrup

¾ cup (150g) sugar

2 Tablespoons butter or margarine, melted

1 teaspoon vanilla extract

1¼ (160g) cups coarsely chopped pecans

Directions

1. Preheat oven to 350 degrees F. Prepare Bar Cookie Crust

2. Meanwhile, in a large bowl beat eggs, corn syrup, sugar, butter and vanilla until well blended. Stir in pecans. Pour over hot crust; spread evenly.

3. Bake 20 minutes or until filling is firm around edges and slightly firm in center. Cool completely on wire rack. Cut into 2 x1½-inch bars

Makes about 32 bars

CHOCOLATE CHIP WALNUT BARS

This holiday cookie is a year-round favorite

1 recipe Bar cookie crust (Recipe page 39)

2 eggs

½ cup (170g) light or dark corn syrup

½ cup (100g) sugar

2 Tablespoons margarine or butter

1 cup (6-oz) semisweet chocolate chips

¼ cup (38g) chopped walnuts

Directions

1. Preheat oven to 350 degrees F. Prepare Bar cookie Crust. Meanwhile, in medium bowl, beat eggs, corn syrup, sugar and margarine until well blended. Stir in chocolate chips and walnuts. Pour over hot crust; spread evenly.

2. Bake 15 to 18 minutes or until set. Cool completely on wire rack. Cut into 2 x 1 ½ -inch bars.

Makes 24 Bars

CRANBERRY WALNUT BARS

Look for dried cranberries in supermarkets or gourmet stores.

1 recipe Bar Cookie Crust (Recipe page 39)

2 eggs

½ cup (170g) light or dark corn syrup

½ cup (100g) sugar

2 Tablespoons margarine or butter, melted

1 cup dried cranberries or raisins (about 6-oz)

¾ cup (100g) chopped walnuts

Directions

1. Preheat oven to 350 degrees F. Prepare Bar cookie crust. Meanwhile, in medium bowl beat eggs, corn syrup, sugar and margarine until well blended. Stir in cranberries and walnuts. Pour over hot crust; spread evenly.

2. Bake 15 to 20 minutes or until set. Cool completely on wire rack. Cut into 2x1 ½ -inch bars.

Makes about 32 bars

ALMOND TOFFEE TRIANGLES

1 Recipe Bar Cookie Crust (Recipe page 39)

½ cup (170g) corn syrup

1/3 cup (73g) packed brown sugar

2 Tablespoons butter or margarine

¼ cup (60ml) heavy or whipping cream

1½ cups (225g) sliced almonds

1 teaspoon vanilla extract

Directions

1. Preheat oven to 350 degrees F. Prepare cookie crust (recipe above)

2. Meanwhile: In a medium saucepan combine corn syrup, brown sugar, butter and cream. Bring to a boil over medium heat; remove from heat. Stir in almonds and vanilla. Pour over hot cookie crust; spread evenly.

3. Bake 12 minutes or until set and golden; cool completely on wire rack. Cut into 2-inch squares; cut diagonally in half for triangles.

Makes 48 triangles

CHOCOLATE RASPBERRY BARS

2 cups (250g) flour, sifted

½ teaspoon baking powder

¼ teaspoon salt

½ cup (113g butter

¼ cup (50g) sugar

2 egg yokes

¼ cup (60ml) water

1 teaspoon vanilla extract

1 cup raspberry jam

1 cup fresh raspberries

Meringue:

3 egg whites

¼ teaspoon salt

½ cup (100g) sugar

1 cup nuts, (130g) finely chopped in processor

Topping:

1 cup (170g) chocolate morsels, melted

Directions

1. Sift together flour, baking powder and salt, Cream butter and gradually add sugar, beat in egg yolks one at a time; add flour alternating with water and vanilla. Press dough in 12 x 12 inch pan.

Bring jam to a boil and fresh berries. Cook one minute and spread over dough.

2. Beat egg whites and salt until stiff, add sugar gradually, and beat until soft peaks form, fold in nuts. Spread over jam and bake at 350° F. for 25 minutes.

3. Drizzle melted chocolate over all. Allow to cool and cut into bars.

Makes about 24 bars.

PEACH STREUSEL BARS

 2 cups (250g) all-purpose flour

½ cup (100g) firmly packed light brown sugar

1 teaspoon grated lemon peel

¼ teaspoon ground nutmeg

¼ teaspoon salt

¾ cup (170g) unsalted butter

1 (12-oz.) jar peach preserves

Directions

1. Preheat oven to 375° F. Grease 9 x 9 x 2-inch square pan. Combine flour, sugar, lemon rind, nutmeg and salt in large bowl. Cut in butter with pastry blender until mixture is crumbly. Reserve 1 cup of mixture. Pat remaining mixture evenly into prepared pan.

2. Spread preserves evenly over dough, leaving ¼-inch border around edge. Sprinkle with reserved flour mixture.

3. Bake for 40 minutes or until lightly browned. Cool in pan on wire rack. Cut into bite-sized bars. Store for up to 1 week in air-tight container. Makes 16 bars.

BUTTER CRUNCH CHEESECAKE BARS

Crust:

3/4 cup (170g) butter, softened

1/3 cup (73g) dark brown sugar

1/3 cup (67g) sugar

2 cups (250g) all-purpose flour

1 cup (122g) (shelled walnuts, chopped

Filling:

2(8-oz 226g) pkg. cream cheese, softened

½ cup sugar

1 teaspoon vanilla extract

 2 eggs

 6 small chocolate crispy peanut butter flavored candy bars (such as Butterfinger), chopped

Directions

1. Heat oven to 350 degrees.

2. Crust: In a bowl, beat butter with mixer until smooth and creamy, about1 min. Add sugars, beat 3 min. until fluffy. Beat in flour. Beat in nuts until just combined. Reserve 1 cup mixture. Press remainder over bottom of ungreased 13x9x2-inch baking pan. Bake crust 10 min. Let cool.

3. Filling: In a bowl, beat together cream cheese and sugar with mixer until smooth. Add vanilla and eggs, beat for 2 minutes. Fold in candy bars. Spoon over baked crust. Sprinkle reserved crust mixture over top.

4. Bake for 30 minutes. Until cheesecake layer is set. Let cool. Cut into 16 bars. Serve, or cover and refrigerate. Makes 16 bars

BUTTERSCOTCH OATMEAL BARS

1¼ (280g) cups all-purpose flour

1 teaspoon baking soda

1 teaspoon ground cinnamon

1 cup butter, softened

¾ cup (150g) white sugar

¾ cup (110 g) packed brown sugar

2 eggs

1 teaspoon vanilla or grated peel of one orange

3 cups (255 g) quick cooking oats

2 cups (340g) butterscotch chips

Directions

1. Preheat oven to 375 degrees F (190C). Grease 15 x 10 inch-pan

2. In a small bowl combine flour, baking soda, and cinnamon; set aside. In large bowl beat butter, sugar, brown sugar, eggs and vanilla in large bowl. Gradually beat in flour mixture. Stir in oats and butterscotch chips. Spread dough into prepared pan. Bake for 18-20 minutes or until very lightly browned.

BOURBON AND MAPLE BARS

1 cup (125g) unbleached all-purpose flour

1 teaspoon Baking powder

1 cup (113g) unsalted butter softened

1 cup (220g) Light brown sugar packed

2 large Eggs

1 teaspoon Vanilla extract

1 cup (340g) Maple syrup

2 Tablespoons Bourbon

1 cup (150g) Pecans or walnuts chopped

Glaze:

1 cup (125g) Confectioners' sugar

2 Tablespoons Maple sugar

2 Tablespoons Bourbon

Directions

1. Preheat the oven to 350 degrees F. Lightly butter a 13 x 9- inch baking pan.

2. To make the Batter: Sift together the flour and baking powder; set aside. In a large bowl, cream the butter and brown sugar with an electric mixer until light and fluffy. Gradually beat in the eggs and vanilla until blended. Combine the maple syrup and bourbon; add in a slow, steady stream, beating gently until blended.

3. Stir in the flour mixture until blended. Add the pecans or walnuts; stir to blend. Spread the batter in the prepared pan. Bake for 35 minutes, or until the edges begin to pull away from the sides of the pan. Cool on a wire rack, and glaze the bars while still warm.

4. To make the Glaze: Shift the confectioners' sugar into a small bowl. In a separate bowl, stir together the maple syrup and bourbon. Add the liquids to the confectioners' sugar, stirring until smooth. Drizzle the glaze over the warm bar cookies, spreading it into a thin, even layer. Cool thoroughly before cutting into bars

Makes 24 bars.

ULTIMATE SOUR LEMON BARS

1½ cups (185g) all-purpose flour

¼ cup (30g) Powdered Sugar

1 Pinch salt

½ cup (113g) unsalted butter, cut Into Pieces

½ teaspoon vanilla extract

Topping:

5 Large eggs -- room temp

2 cups (400g) sugar

1 cup (300ml) lemon juice,

3 Tablespoons all-purpose flour

2½ Tablespoons grated lemon peel

Directions

1. Preheat oven to 350ºF. Line 9" square pan with foil, extending 1" above sides of pan. Grease uncovered 2 sides of pan.

2. Combine flour, powdered sugar and salt in food processor. Add butter and cut in using on/off turns until mixture appears sandy. Add vanilla and process until dough begins to come together. Press evenly into prepared pan. Bake until golden brown, about 26 to 28 minutes.

3. Meanwhile, prepare topping: Whisk eggs and 2 Cups sugar in medium bowl to blend. Whisk in lemon juice, add flour. Strain into another bowl. Mix in grated lemon peel. Reduce oven to 325ºF. Pour filling over hot crust. Bake until sides are set and filling no longer moves in center when pan is shaken, about 2 to 22 minutes cool on rack.

4. Cover and chill at least 4 hours. Using foil sides too, lift dessert from pan. Fold down foil sides. Cut into 16 squares. Cut each square diagonally in half, forming triangles. Sift top with additional powdered sugar.

Makes 32 Bars

CARMEL-OATS CANDY BAR

1 (14-oz.) package caramel candies, unwrapped

1/3 (80ml) cup milk

2 cups (500g) unbleached flour

2 cups (170g) quick-cooking or regular oats

1½ cups (330g) packed brown sugar

1 teaspoon baking soda

½ teaspoon salt

1 large egg

1 cup (113g) margarine or butter, softened

1 (6-oz) package semisweet chocolate chips

1 cup (122g) chopped walnuts or dry roasted peanuts

Directions

1. Preheat oven to 350 degrees F. Grease a 13 x 9 x 2-inch baking pan.

2. In 2-quart saucepan heat candies and milk over low heat, stirring frequently, until smooth; remove from heat. In a large bowl combine flour, oats, brown sugar, baking soda, salt and egg; mix well. Stir in margarine with fork until mixture is crumbly. Press half of the crumbly mixture in pan. Bake 10 minutes. Sprinkle with chocolate chips and walnuts; drizzle with caramel mixture. Sprinkle remaining crumbly mixture over top.

3. Bake until golden brown, 20 to 25 minutes. Cool 30 minutes. Loosen edges from sides of pan; cool completely. Cut into 2 x 1-inch bars. Makes about 52 bars

MAPLE PECAN BARS

Coconut-Graham Layer:

1¼ cups (300g) graham-cracker crumbs

1¼ cups (190g) finely ground pecans

1¼ cups (90g) shredded sweetened coconut

1¼ cups (200g) semisweet chocolate pieces

6 Tablespoons (84g) unsalted butter, at room temperature

Maple-Cream Layer:

3 cups (500g) confectioners' sugar

½ cup (1 stick 113g) unsalted butter, at room temperature

1/3 cup (113g) maple syrup

Chocolate Topping

8 squares (1 oz. each) semisweet chocolate, chopped

1 cup (240ml) heavy cream

2 ounces (28g) white chocolate, chopped

Directions

1. Graham Layer: Combine crumbs, pecans, coconut, chocolate and butter in bowl. Press evenly over bottom of 13 x 9 x 2-inch baking dish. Refrigerate 30 minutes.

2. Maple-Cream Layer: Beat powdered sugar, butter and maple syrup in bowl until smooth and creamy. Spread evenly over graham layer. Refrigerate until firm, about 2 hours.

3. Topping: Melt semisweet chocolate in cream in saucepan over low heat. Cool to room temperature, about 20 minutes. Pour evenly over maple layer. Refrigerate until firm, for about 3 hours.

4. Melt white chocolate in small saucepan over low heat. Cool slightly. Drizzle over Chocolate Topping. Refrigerate until set, about 10 minutes. Cut into 24 two-inch squares; cut each square in half for 48 bars. Freeze or refrigerate.

Makes 4 dozen cookie bars

GUMDROP COOKIE BARS
2 cups (500g) flour

1 cup (8-oz.) chopped gumdrops

½ cup (75g) chopped pecans

4 eggs

1 Tablespoon water

2 cups (440g) packed brown sugar

1 teaspoon cinnamon

¼ teaspoon salt

3 Tablespoons (42g) butter, softened

1 Teaspoon grated orange peel

2 Tablespoons orange juice

Powdered Sugar

Directions

1. Preheat oven to 375 degrees F. grease 15 ½ x 10 ½ pan

2. Mix together flour, gumdrops and pecans; set aside. In a medium bowl, beat together eggs and water. Add brown sugar and beat until it is just light. Beat in cinnamon and salt. Stir gumdrop mixture into the brown sugar mixture. Spread into a. Bake in preheated oven until cookies are done, about 15 to 18 minutes.

3. For Icing: In saucepan, melt 3 Tablespoons of butter over low heat. Remove from heat and add 1 teaspoon of great orange peel and 2 tablespoons of orange juice. Sift in enough powdered sugar to make a thin icing and blend until smooth. Spread icing over warm cookies and cut into bars.

FUDGY MINT BROWNIES
¼ cup (57g) margarine, softened

2/3 cup (134g) sugar

2 egg whites, divided

2 Tablespoon water

2 teaspoons vanilla extract

¾ cup (96g) all-purpose flour

¼ teaspoon baking powder

1/3 cup (40g) unsweetened cocoa

8 peppermint candy pieces, finely crushed

Vegetable cooking spray

Directions

1. Beat margarine with an electric mixer at medium speed until creamy; gradually add sugar, beating well. Add egg whites, water and vanilla; beat well.

2. Combine flour, baking powder, cocoa and candy; add to margarine mixture, stirring just until dry ingredients are moistened; set aside.

3. Pour into an 8-in square pan coated with vegetable spray. Bake: at 350 degrees F. for 22 to 24 minutes or until edges pull away from pan slightly. Cool in pan on a wire rack.

Makes 16 Brownies

CHOCOLATE MINT BROWNIES

 If you can't find mint chocolate chips for the topping, use semi-sweet chocolate chips with a few drops of mint extract.

Base

1 cup (125g) all-purpose flour

½ cup (113g) butter, softened

½ teaspoon salt

4 large eggs

1 teaspoon vanilla extract

1 (16-oz.) can chocolate-flavored syrup

1 cup granulated sugar

For the filling:

2 cups (250g) powdered sugar

½ cup (113g) butter, softened

1 Tablespoon water

½ teaspoon mint extract

3 drops green food coloring

For the topping:

1 (10-ounce) package mint chocolate chips

9 Tablespoons (127g) butter

Directions

1. Preheat oven to 350 degrees F. Grease 13 x 9 x 2-inch baking pan.

2. Combine the ingredients for the base in a large mixing bowl; beat at medium speed for 3 minutes. Pour batter into prepared baking pan. Bake for 30 minutes (top of brownies will still appear wet). Cool completely.

3. To make the filling: Combine filling ingredients in a medium mixing bowl; beat until creamy. Spread over cooled brownies. Refrigerate until set.

4. To make the topping: Melt chocolate chips and butter over low heat in a small saucepan (then add mint extract, if using). Let cool for 30 minutes or until lukewarm, stirring occasionally. Spread over filling. Chill before cutting. Store in the refrigerator.

Makes about 60 bars

RASPBERRY AND WALNUT SHORTBREAD

1¼ cups (160g) plus 2 Tablespoons flour, divided

½ cup (100g) granulated sugar

½ cup (113g) butter or margarine

½ cup raspberry jam

2 eggs

½ cup (90g) brown sugar

1 teaspoon vanilla

1/8 teaspoon salt

1/8 teaspoon baking soda

1 cup (128g) walnuts or pecans

Directions

1. Preheat oven to 350 degrees F. lightly greased 9 x9-inch baking pan

2. In medium bowl combine 1¼ cups flour and sugar. With a pastry blender or two knives, cut butter into dry ingredients until mixture resembles coarse crumbles. Press into bottom of prepared 9x9-inch baking pan.

3. Bake in preheated oven for 20 minutes or until edges are lightly golden. Remove from oven; spread raspberry jam over shortbread.

4. In medium bowl beat eggs, brown sugar, and vanilla until creamy. Combine 2 Tablespoons flour, salt and soda, add to egg mixture and stir to blend. Stir in walnuts. Spoon over jam, spreading lightly to corners of pan.

5. Bake in preheated oven for 20 minutes more or until top is set. Cool in pan, cut into bars.

CHOCOLATE ALMOND SHORTBREAD

¾ cup (170g) butter or margarine, softened

6 squares semisweet chocolate, melted, cooled

1 teaspoon vanilla extract

1 cup (125g) all-purpose flour

1 cup (122g) toasted ground blanched almonds

¼ teaspoon salt

½ cup (71g) toasted chopped almonds

Directions

1. Preheat oven to 350 degrees F.

Beat butter and sugar until light and fluffy. Stir in chocolate and vanilla. Mix in flour, ground almonds and salt

2. Press dough into 12x9-inch rectangle ungreased cookie sheet. Sprinkle with chopped almonds; press lightly into dough.

3. Bake for 45 to 50 minutes or until set. Cool on cookie sheet. Cut into bars

Makes 36 bars

ALMOND-ORANGE SHORTBREAD

1 cup (128g) sliced almonds, divided

2 cups (250g) all-purpose flour

1 cup (226g) cold butter, cut into pieces

½ cup (100g) sugar

½ cup (64g) cornstarch

2 Tablespoons grated orange peel

1 teaspoon extract

Directions

1. Preheat oven to 350 degrees F.

2. To toast almonds, spread ¾ cup almonds in a single layer in a large baking sheet. Bake 6 minutes or until golden brown, stirring frequently. Remove almonds from oven. Cool completely in pan. Reduce oven temperature to 325 degrees F.

3. Place almonds in a food processor. Process using on/off pulsing action until almonds are coarsely chopped. Add flour, butter, sugar, cornstarch, orange peel and almond extract. Process using on/off pulsing action until mixture resembles coarse crumbs.

4. Press dough firmly and evenly into 10 ½ x 8 ½ rectangle or large ungreased baking sheet. Score dough into 1 ¼-inch squares. Press one slice of remaining ½ cup almonds in center of each square.

5. Bake 30 to 40 minutes or until shortbread is firm when pressed and lightly browned. Immediately cut into squares along score lines. Remove cookies with a spatula to wire racks; cool completely. Store loosely covered at room temperature up to 1 week. Makes 5 dozen cookies.

Conclusion

Thank You for purchasing Ultimate Christmas Cookies. My grandchildren and I have had a lot of fun baking and testing the recipes. I hope you have also enjoyed the recipes and found some new family favorites.

Contents

LEMON SUGAR COOKIES 28

SNOWMEN COOKIES 29

GRANOLA MERINGUE COOKIES 30

MARSHMALLOW MUD SQUARES 31

FROSTED PUMPKIN SQUARES 32

APPLE CRUMB SQUARES 34

CREAMY LEMON BARS 35

PEANUTTY CHOCOLATE CHIP BARS 36

CHIPPY CHEWY BARS 37

EASY LINZER BARS 38

COOKIE BAR CRUST 39

PECAN PIE BARS 40

CHOCOLATE CHIP WALNUT BARS 41

CRANBERRY WALNUT BARS 42

ALMOND TOFFEE TRIANGLES 43

CHOCOLATE RASPBERRY BARS 44

PEACH STREUSEL BARS 45

BUTTER CRUNCH CHEESECAKE BARS 46

BUTTERSCOTCH OATMEAL BARS 47

BOURBON AND MAPLE BARS 48

ULTIMATE SOUR LEMON BARS 50

CARMEL-OATS CANDY BAR 52

MAPLE PECAN BARS 53

GUMDROP COOKIE BARS 54

FUDGY MINT BROWNIES 55

CHOCOLATE MINT BROWNIES 56

RASPBERRY AND WALNUT SHORTBREAD 58

CHOCOLATE ALMOND SHORTBREAD 59

ALMOND-ORANGE SHORTBREAD 60

Printed in Great Britain
by Amazon